encounters with the Lord

where human frailty meets the sovereignty of God

valerie hoffman

HIGH BRIDGE BOOKS
HOUSTON

Encounters with the Lord
by Valerie Hoffman

Copyright © 2022 Valerie Hoffman

All rights reserved.

Printed in the United States of America
ISBN: 978-1-954943-31-5

All rights reserved. Except in the case of brief quotations embodied in critical articles and reviews, no portion of this book may be reproduced, stored in a retrieval system, or transmitted in any form or by any means—electronic, mechanical, photocopy, recording, scanning, or other—without prior written permission from the author.

High Bridge Books titles may be purchased in bulk for educational, business, fundraising, or sales promotional use. For information, please contact High Bridge Books via www.HighBridgeBooks.com/contact.

Photographs copyright © 2022 Gregg Stuessi

Published in Houston, Texas, by High Bridge Books.

acknowledgments

I want to acknowledge Paul Hoffman, who reflected the person of the Lord Jesus Christ and displayed His Love in life and also in death.

Your illness was the instrument used by our Lord and Savior to prepare me for the path I still have to walk without you.

You were always my rock, Paul Hoffman.

contents

preface _____ vii

1. the beat of my heart _____ 1
2. channel of love _____ 3
3. my constellations _____ 7
4. clenched fists _____ 9
5. mountain heights and valley depths _____ 13
6. battle at midpoint _____ 17
7. hidden treasures _____ 19
8. measured time _____ 23
9. refined _____ 27
10. the footprint _____ 31
11. the Man at the gate _____ 35
12. child of the light _____ 39
13. trapped in my castle _____ 43
14. the Artisan's touch _____ 47
15. Morning Star _____ 51
16. escaping trouble _____ 55
17. longing to be seen _____ 59
18. clay in Your hands _____ 63
19. giants at the door _____ 67
20. loose gravel _____ 71
21. elusive hope _____ 75

22. ashes for beauty	79
23. what lies between us	83
24. the Light Bearer's hiding place	87
25. the waiting room	91
26. opposing forces	95
27. abiding	99
28. depths of discontentment	103
29. manifested miracles	107
30. just out of reach	111
31. undertow	115
32. the intersection	119
33. stolen dreams	123
34. the embellishment	127
35. broken pieces	131
36. the tomb	135
37. the healing	139
38. the prison	143
39. no limits	147
40. the silence	151
41. the Gardener	155
42. living waters	159

preface

I speak to those struggling in the despairs of life, when human comfort cannot pierce the anguish. Pain will either consume you or usher you into an intersection with the Sovereign God—a convergence of suffering and redemptive Love.

Let's walk together along your dark path, where I will introduce you to the God-Man, who offers Grace and Mercy in your time of hopelessness. Let me be your voice when words betray you. Come, let us encounter the Lord Jesus Christ together.

These devotions were born out of a five-year journey in a barren wilderness of deep lamenting as I watched my husband physically decline unto death. In the middle of my emotional pain and mental anguish, the Lord was strengthening my weak hands and feeble knees. I began to realize that God was fortifying my fearful heart and shaping me into His vessel of purpose through redemptive suffering as I encountered Him on a daily basis. My eyes began to observe things blooming in soil that was dying. My parched and thirsty ground became springs of water as I pursued the Lord Jesus Christ.

I stand as a witness that if you invite the Sovereign God of the universe to walk with you along your journey, you can endure your hardship and come out on the other side in a place you never thought possible. Trust His Goodness, knowing He has a plan and purpose for you on the other side of your circumstances. That purpose might be right in front of you but hidden from your sight. Or it might be something you could never imagine that is still yet to unfold.

Do not resist your despair; instead, let it arise to enrich your life and lead you to restoration. Drink from the cup of suffering so you can taste redemption and worship the One and Only True God.

special thanks

Sometimes the Lord calls us to embark upon adventures too large for us to dream, causing retreat within a barrage of impossibilities. But if your heart dares to wonder, the Lord will bring special people to embolden you and provide the necessary support. I want to thank the many people who verbally affirmed my writing, which encouraged me to keep going. However, one person has yielded innumerable hours editing and providing technical support. Paula Oestreich, I would not be at this point without your unyielding support and encouragement throughout my writing and blogging adventure. You have my undying love and gratitude.

Now let me speak directly to the photographer whose masterful eye is behind all the photography associated with each story, Gregg Stuessi. I am not only captivated by your art but honored that you have joined with me, adding another visual layer to my writing. I am grateful for you and thankful that you are my brother.

1

the beat of my heart

"I am walking down a scary path, Lord. I do not know where it leads and what the outcome will bring. This course contains not only my life but the welfare of someone else whose well-being is in my hands. I feel lost and unsure; worry is seeping through the hairline cracks in my soul."

"Look at Me, my darling," the Lord said in a soft voice.

As I turned to look upon the face of my Savior, our eyes met and His Peace flooded every tissue of my being with His Living Water.

Taking my hand and placing it in the center of His chest, Jesus said, "Feel the beat of My heart and let your anxious ways be calmed to My rhythm. Feel My Peace consume you, for it will guard your heart and mind always. Receive what I have for you, My child."

"You cause a new song to rise up from within me, Lord. Make me rest in Your Love."

Comforted by Philippians 4:4-7; John 4:10; John 14:27

2

channel of love

"My flesh appears to have broken free of its reins and is running amuck, murmuring about my situation and manifesting ugly traits that I do not even recognize. I am starting to feel there is no point to this suffering, Lord."

"There is always a point to your suffering," said the Lord. "Right now, you are being presented with an opportunity to exhibit the highest form of love, sacrificial love. But it will mandate that you lay aside your own needs and desires to suffer for someone else's benefit."

Looking down at the floor, I responded, "That type of love sounds heroic, Lord. I am not sure I have it in me. I often stumble under the pressure of this trial, which causes me to feel more shame and anger than love. How can I give something I do not have to give?"

"Do not miss this chance to portray God's love because of your own feelings of inadequacy," replied the Lord. "I am the channel of love that flows from the Heavenly Father. I chose you and will not forsake the work of My hands. You can do this because of Me. When you dwell with Me, that channel is kept open and flowing freely, which will enable you to love others. Trust in My abilities, not in yours. I will perfect what is lacking in you, and that is the purpose for your troubles."

"Lord, forgive my selfish heart and strengthen my inner being with power so You may dwell in my heart through faith. I trust You to perfect what is lacking in me. Keep me rooted and grounded in Your Love so I can love others through my words and actions.

Comforted by John 15; Psalm 138:8; Ephesians 3:16-17; 1 John 3:16-18; 1 John 4:8; 1 Peter 5:10

3

my constellations

"As I breathe in the night air and watch the skies turn to midnight blue, the starry hosts ready themselves for their nightly performance. At the sound of Your voice, as You call each star by name, the curtain is pulled back and they enter the stage for all to witness. Not one of them is missing, for they are contained by Your great Power and Mighty Strength, Lord."

But as I exhale and take in my very next breath, my attention falls from the spans of glory to my circumstances, taking my thoughts from beauty to beast.

"My constellations tell a story for all to hear and observe," said the Lord. "You are in My theatre spotlight for audience observation. I know the plot is tragic and unwelcomed, but I am setting the scene to display My intervention in your life. Collaborate with Me; ready yourself and listen for My voice when I call your name. Come forth center stage and shine for Me."

"Yes, Lord. Ready my ears for when You call my name. May I come forth shining like a star in the canopy of Your Heavenly tent? You are the Creator of the ends of the earth, possessing great Power and mighty Strength. I trust You to contain my circumstances and sustain me throughout this battle. Thank you for Your unfailing love."

Comforted by Isaiah 40:26

4
clenched fists

"I am clutching Your promises in my hand, Lord. They are the only thing pushing me forward into tomorrow. My soul and the wellness of my heart lie in Your palms."

The Lord's hands enclosed around mine, gently moving my clenched fists over my heart. "Hold tight to My promises while waiting for their fulfillment. Keep them hidden deep inside your heart so they can take root."

Staring into His kind face, I replied, "The uncertainty of this battle makes me anxious for the future, concerned for what it holds for me, Lord."

"Your struggle tugs at My heart, but those difficulties will allow Me to work within a seemingly impossible situation. There must be unfortunate things in life to contrast the good I will bring from it. Trust Me with your future and everything that unfolds until that day arrives."

Holding me in His arms as I sobbed, the Lord said, "Be confident of My Words and rest in My hope—wait patiently for what you do not yet have. None of My Words will ever fail, My dear child. Remain close to Me, and I will strengthen your heart. Remember, I always see you and hear you."

"Intercede for me in my weakness, Lord. Strengthen my resolve. Lead me to special people who will encourage and assist me in nurturing the promises I hold in my heart. May I be found worthy of Your trust, Lord, as I wait for the fulfillment of the words You have spoken to me."

Comforted by Romans 8:24-25, 28; Psalm 33:18; Psalm 31:24

5

mountain heights and valley depths

Dawn is breaking, and doubts start rising on the horizon of my heart. My spirit lifts with the possibility of a miracle emerging with a new day, but my soul is hiding a secret hope that my hard service might be completed.

"I will lower the height of the mountain," said the Lord, "and raise the depth of the valley, but you still need to make the climb. The ascent will be difficult, but I will help you reach the peak. You will find that I have smoothed the rugged ground so you can withstand the hardship."

Burdened with shame, I cried, "I want to be convinced that You will fulfill what You have promised, Lord. But my heart struggles to believe at times. My life experiences tip the scales in the opposite direction, making me struggle to see where You are working in the mess of my life. Please help my unbelief, Lord."

The Lord moved closer, drawn to my humble brokenness, and said, "My Words will never pass away, and they are completely reliable; you will do well to pay attention to them. Cry out to Me from your desert, and I will gather you into My arms. When you are approaching the summit and cannot press on, I will carry you close to My heart until we reach the mountaintop together. Remember My Words, for My mouth has spoken them."

"You are the Shepherd & Overseer of my soul, Lord. I will trust You as I scale the mountain. Direct me to Your Words and help me claim them with confidence. For You have spoken them, Lord."

Comforted by Isaiah 40:1-5, 11; Matthew 24:35; Psalm 34:18; 1 Peter 2:25

6

battle at midpoint

"My days are filled with unforeseen surprises, Lord—the kind of events that are never pleasant and often carry the message "but what if," a message packed with an invisible force of temptation, taunting me to succumb to the uncertainty, all under the disguise of another mislaid dream. I feel lost in the middle of an unending cycle of desperation."

"There are no surprises with Me." said the Lord. "I am the beginning and the ending of all things, seen and unseen. I also occupy the middle. Nothing exists without Me because I hold all things together."

"I am not holding together very well, Lord. How does my anguish fit into Your perfect cycle of existence?" I asked.

"There is a battle at midpoint, where you reside," said the Lord. "But I have gone before you and will cause My Goodness to pass in front of you. Stand on the Rock as I fight for you so you can witness My Glory in the center of your despair. I am perfecting you. Yield to My creative work; do not resist it nor try to speed it up."

"Cause me to humbly fall into Your redemptive work, Lord God. Give me eyes to see Your Glory and Goodness in the middle of my battle. You are my Rock, Lord, and I will take refuge in You."

Comforted by Revelation 1:8; Colossians 1:16; Exodus 33:18-21; James 1:4; Psalm 94:22; Romans 8:28

7

hidden treasures

I am covered in dirt as I comb through the rubble of my life, seeking to find any familiar remnant from the crumbled walls of normalcy. Wiping my eyes, I catch a glimmer of something shiny buried under the wreckage.

Reaching down and brushing away the dust, I discover a lovely trinket, unknown to me. A little bewildered, I whisper to myself, "I wonder where this came from?"

"I placed it there, " said the Lord. "It is My hidden treasure just for you: beauty in exchange for ashes."

I felt the worth of the possession rise in my heart, and it became invaluable to me. As I looked around the room for a container to keep the item safe, my thoughts were interrupted by the Lord.

"I created a special storage place for your treasures, My dear. It is your heart. I will fill the treasure chest of those who love Me, but be attentive to what you store inside. Your treasures and your heart are linked together. Wherever one is, you will find the other. I have set you as the ruler over your treasury; preserve the treasures that I give you and release the ransom of this world. Be wise with what you store in the secret place of your heart."

"All the treasures of wisdom and knowledge are hidden in You, Lord Jesus. Give me a clean heart so when I pour out its contents before You, the bounty is found pleasing in Your sight."

Comforted by Isaiah 61:3; Isaiah 45:3; 1 Chronicles 26:22; Matthew 6:20-21; Proverbs 8:21; Psalm 62:8; Colossians 2:3

8

measured time

I feel trapped between yesterday and tomorrow, trying to make sense of today. On the one hand, life is painfully slow, but on the other, it is barreling toward an ending that appears to be inevitable, casting me into an eerie time warp.

"Time lies within My hand," declared the Lord. Moving toward the windows overlooking the forest, He continued, "In the beginning, I laid the foundations of the earth and created the Heavens. I have always been in existence, but human interpretation of time is measured by the cycles of My sun, moon, and stars. Your duration and destiny fall within My plan."

"Every day brings such a struggle. It all seems unproductive, just going through the motions with no beneficial outcome in sight," I said with a hint of hopelessness in my voice.

Jesus took my hand in His. Waiting for our eyes to meet, He said, "Nothing is wasted, My dear. There is a time to every purpose, and your present suffering cannot be compared with the glory that will be revealed in you. I formed your spirit and prepare a place for you in My Kingdom. Humble yourself under My hand and love wisely, for your set time to rejoice will come."

"You sit enthroned forever, and my soul praises You, Lord Jesus. I rejoice in Your Righteousness and trust in Your faithfulness to complete what You have started in me."

Comforted by Genesis 1; Psalm 102:13, 25; Zechariah 12:1; Matthew 25:34; 1 Peter 5:6; Romans 8:18; Ephesians 5:16; Ecclesiastes 3:1; Proverbs 31:25

9

refined

"I am questioning my abilities as this trial keeps unfolding, Lord. It feels as though I am missing the mark at every turn, falling short of my expectations, becoming a judge in my own court of self-condemnation."

"What do you see?" asked Jesus, sitting on His throne. The question ushered my mind into overdrive, quickly identifying certain failures, some real and some perceived, each one looking back at me with contempt.

My thoughts were interrupted when Jesus declared, "I delivered Myself unto death, freeing you from all condemnation. You belong to Me. Yes, maybe your offenses are many, but My Grace is greater and abounds. Through Me, the only true Judge, you have been justified to live abundantly. Do you really want to reject My free gift of Grace and put yourself back under bondage?"

"No, Lord, I do not," I said with a sigh, stepping down from my imaginary judge's bench.

"Place all your transgressions in this container at my feet," said Jesus as He reached down to open the box's lid.

I noticed it was stained with His blood, and written across the top was the word *Refined*.

As I placed my guilt-laden sins inside the chest, the Lord said, "This container belongs to Me, and the contents are Mine. Do not attempt to take back what now belongs to Me. Sin will deceitfully hold you captive, forcing you to yield to its ways, causing spiritual death. But I have freed you from its power and made you alive unto God. When there is a new offense, place it in My hands, making room in your heart for what is pure. Walk in the newness of life to which you have been called."

"Thank you for Your great compassion, Lord. For it is You who has blotted out my transgressions, washing away all my iniquity and cleansing me from my sin. Cause me to always call upon You out of a pure heart, Lord, enabling me to see You."

Comforted by Romans 4:25, 5:4-20, 6:4-23, 7:6-23, 8:1 & 15; Galatians 4:3; John 3:17; 1 John 1:7; Matthew 5:8; Psalm 51:1-2; Psalm 75:7; 1 Corinthians 6:20

10

the footprint

Pulling my injured foot from a salt bath, I noticed a perfect image of my footprint resting on the bottom of the black metal pot. Not trusting what I saw, I reached down to stir the water. To my surprise, the faint impression of my foot would fade in and out, disappearing and reappearing with the water's movement and the light's reflection.

As I marveled at the molecular interaction, the Lord interjected, "I crafted your DNA and set your genetic code to form your individual blueprint. You are My created masterpiece. I know the unique pattern of your footprint, every ridge on your fingerprint, and the curves of your face. You have been set apart for My purposes."

"I marvel at Your Love while humbled that You created me to be unique. What purpose do You have for me, Lord?" I asked.

"You are made in My image," the Lord answered, "specifically crafted to reflect your Maker for the world to witness. Those beautiful feet of yours were made to carry My Peace and good tidings to others. But there will be a day when I will receive unto Myself your last breath, ushering you into My presence, where I have a mansion prepared for you. I was joyful in My creation of you, but I also delight in bringing you home to Me."

"May I be found faithful in the purposes You have for me, Lord. Enable my feet to always carry Your message of Love and Peace while reflecting Your image to the world."

Comforted by John 1:1-5, 4:13,14:2-3; Psalm 139:14; Galatians 1:15-16; Romans 10:15; Genesis 2:7; Hebrews 1:1-4; Romans 11:36; Ecclesiastes 3:2; 2 Corinthians 5:8; Psalm 116:15

11

the Man at the gate

This decision is too much for me. Closing my eyes to rest my mind, I soon found myself running down a narrow tree-lined path. Something was chasing me, and the horror I felt seemed real. Shadows began casting their long images over the pathway, but I noticed a Light in the distance. I kept pushing toward that Light until the trail emptied into a courtyard and my feet landed at the threshold of a gate.

A Man whose eyes were filled with Light was standing at the post of the gateway. Smiling, He said to me, "I saw you coming from a long way off. The winds of your storm have captured your sweet-smelling fragrance, filling the air. The aroma pleases Me greatly."

Collapsing on my side of the gate, I could only sob.

"What is your request of Me?" He asked.

Standing to my feet and raising my eyes to meet His, I whispered, "I do not know what to do, Lord. My husband has reached a point of decline where I need to determine the next steps. No option is a good one, but what is the best option, Lord? I cannot make this decision on my own. I need You to show me what is the right decision."

"People plan their lives," the Lord answered, "but they never know their own way because I am the One who directs their steps."

Still standing in the courtyard, the Lord swung open the gate that stood between us. Extending His right hand toward me, the Lord said, "Take My hand and walk with Me."

Stepping over the threshold, we entered a spacious garden. I felt peace come over me as the Lord said, "I know this journey seems bleak, but I will not leave you alone. I will guide you and help you along the way, bringing about success in all you do. Take refuge in Me. I will be with you for the duration, watching over you and guiding you back into a fruitful land."

"My heart is etched with Your Words and drawn to Your Love, Lord. May I be found entering in at the King's gate of Righteousness, sitting at Your feet with thanksgiving. Strengthen my resolve as I trust in Your provision and guidance."

Comforted by Esther 5:1-3; Philippians 4:18; Song of Solomon 1:12; Psalm 118:19-21; John 10:9; Genesis 28:15; Hebrews 13:5; Romans 8:28; Proverbs 20:24

12

child of the light

The snowstorm has caused the atmosphere to become thick in a composition of white, gray, and black—colorless, like the canvas of my soul. Out of nowhere, a beam of light cuts through the clouds, radiating in a spectrum of colors.

"I know that is You, manifesting Your glorious presence, Lord. Thank You for being present with me in my pain," I said, wiping tears from my cheek.

"Your spirit is so heavy; what is weighing down your heart?" the Lord asked rhetorically, fully aware of all things hidden.

Looking down at the ground, not proud of my answer, I said, "I have no peace in my heart, Lord." After a short hesitation, I continued, "I know You are the Prince of Peace, but I can't seem to keep my heart calm. It keeps getting tangled in the reality of this world."

Looking at me with His kind eyes, the Lord said, "I offer My perfect Peace to those who choose to abide in Me, but you must make room for My Words in your heart. My Peace will keep your heart and mind secure when nothing in life makes sense."

Moving toward me, Jesus placed His arm around my shoulder and continued talking while we strolled along the path. "Cling to Me, for there are forces that will try to steal your peace."

"I can sense my peace start to fade when I fill my heart with other things, allowing darkness to encroach," I confessed.

"Ah," the Lord said with a smile. "Do not be troubled by this, for I am also the True Light, which lights every person that comes into the world. All darkness must bow in My presence, and it obeys My Word. Stay in My Light and you will be flooded with the Light that gives understanding."

Turning to face me, the Lord said with a more serious tone, "Stay close to Me so you can fulfill what I have called you to do. I have placed you in the middle of this crooked and perverse nation, where you can shine as My Light despite your pain. You are My prism set high on a hill, bending My Light and dispersing a rainbow of colors that cannot be hidden. I am spellbound by your beauty of obedience, for it pleases Me. Continue to follow Me, and you will not walk in darkness but will have My Light of Life."

"You are my Light and my Salvation, the Strength of my life, Lord. May I bring You honor and glorify our Father in Heaven as I walk as a child of the Light. I pray Your face shines upon me and Your Peace rules in my heart at all times."

Comforted by John 1:9, 8:12, 12:46, 14:27; Isaiah 9:6, 26:3; Matthew 5:14-16; Philippians 2:15, 4:7; Psalm 36:9, 45:11, 119:130.

13

trapped in my castle

Some days I feel like Cinderella, imprisoned in a bad story that has me bogged down with labor and dressed in rags. I married my prince, but he is now deteriorating before my eyes.

Peering out the window and feeling trapped in my castle, I thought to myself, *Can anyone see the silent pain that I carry deep inside? I need someone to hold me tight.*

The room was quiet, lit only by the morning sun spilling through the glass. The silence was broken when I heard a Man's voice behind me, "I see you and your pain."

When I turned, Jesus was standing there. The room was filled with the Power of His presence, mingled with compassion. Holding out His right hand, the Lord said, "Join your hand in Mine and dance with Me."

Captivated by His gesture, I moved toward Jesus. All anxiety melted away as we began swaying to the soft melody that He was singing over me. Consumed with unspeakable joy, I began to twirl like a ballerina.

Smiling at my child-like faith, the Lord said, "Look down at your garment, for I have adorned you with My glorious robe of Righteousness. Your jewels sparkle as you spin in joyful abandonment. Rest in My Love, for I rejoice over you, My dear."

My heart racing, still swept up in the moment, I said, "You have shown me the wonders of Your Love, and my heart delights in You. Will You meet with me again tomorrow, Lord?"

Looking at me with eyes that pierced my soul, the Lord said, "I will hear you in the morning when you call My name. Wait expectantly, for I will come to you."

Comforted by Genesis 16:13; Isaiah 61:10; Zephaniah 3:17; Psalm 5:3, 34:15

14

the Artisan's touch

My life feels like an unfinished piece of artwork, Lord. A canvas propped up on its easel, yet set aside—full of potential, but colorless as I wait for the Artisan's touch.

"I have not set you aside," said the Lord. "On the contrary, for you are a work in progress. I am dry brushing tangles of deception from your mind and blotting out misdeeds that will interfere with your experiences of Me. I am preparing you to receive the colors of your calling."

Hanging my head, I responded, "I do not want anything to stand between You and me."

Knowing the real concern in my heart, the Lord moved toward me. Lifting my chin to meet His eyes, Jesus said, "Nothing and no one can separate you from My Love. Before I formed the worlds, I knew you. Your name has always been on My lips; I even spoke while you were in your mother's womb. I know you well, and I will finish what I started in you."

Pausing long enough to let His Truth take hold, I confessed, "When I am quiet, I can sense Your gentle brush strokes applying watercolors to the fabric of my soul."

"Yes, and not just any palette," the Lord explained. "I have carefully selected the colors displayed on your banner. These pigments have been blended with the vapor of My breath, mixed with My Power, and washed over you. You are My masterpiece, and your final unveiling is yet to come, My darling."

"I am humbled by Your Lovingkindness and Mercy, Lord. Help me stand firm in Your Love as You complete Your work in me. I have put my hope in You and will rejoice in Your salvation as my colorful banner flies in Your name."

Comforted by Isaiah 49:1; Psalm 51:1, 139:13-16, 20:5; Jeremiah 1:5; Romans 8:38-39; Matthew 26:28; 1 Corinthians 6:11; Ephesians 5:26; Song of Solomon 2:4; Philippians 1:6; Revelation 4:11

15

Morning Star

As I watch the sun break the horizon, quietly announcing its arrival, I wonder what today has to offer. As I moved away from the windows, still lost in my thoughts, my words broke the silence, "I sense a change coming, Lord."

"Nothing in My creation remains unchanged," the Lord replied as He moved toward me, hearing the concern in my voice.

"Small changes I can handle, but life-altering events blind me to the familiar things that bring me comfort," I confessed, feeling embarrassed.

Placing His hand under my chin, Jesus gently raised my head, wiping the tears from my cheek. "Keep your eyes focused on Me, the familiar Rock in your life. You know Me. I have never changed, and I never will. In the midst of continual chaos, I AM your one constant. I will not leave you nor allow you to be shaken as the world shifts around you."

Pulling me close to rest my head on His chest, the Lord continued, "I am the bright Morning Star that will return for you. My plan is unfolding, and you are at the center of that plan. Every morning is a reminder for you to watch, for time ticks to My specific tempo, creating the pace to reveal My plan. Stay close, for I will return soon."

Opening my eyes, I found the room empty. I whispered, "I am watching and praying. Come quickly, my Lord!"

Comforted by Malachi 3:6; 1 Corinthians 10:4; Exodus 3:14; Hebrews 13:5,8; John 10:14; Mark 13:32-36; Revelation 22:20-21; Jeremiah 29:11; Psalm 55:22

16

escaping trouble

Today, I have no fight left in my limbs. My energy is spent from fighting these daily battles. I just want to give up and raise my white flag. Continuing to ponder that idea, sitting in my frustration, I wondered what a day with no problems would actually look like.

A voice entered my mind, riding the waves of that thought, saying, "You do not deserve this trouble. Why not just escape from all this misery?"

The voice was familiar, but it was not my own thought.

The tongue of the Tempter continued, "Let me ease your pain. I can keep you out of this blazing furnace; just bow to my *god of easy*."

Shaking my head and snapping to attention, I protested out loud, "No. I will not take what you are offering. My Lord has told me that I will have trouble in this world, but He will give me the strength to push through, delivering me from all my distresses. Jesus will hold me strong, and that is what I will stand on."

The spiritual tension in the room was wrapped with a heavy blanket of silence when I suddenly felt the Lord's presence behind me. His authoritative voice split the air, commanding attention. "This woman belongs to Me, and she has claimed My Name. Now leave."

The Deceiver vanished upon the Lord's charge, the oppression leaving with him.

I turned to face my Savior and threw myself into His arms, leaning on His Love and Faithfulness.

Gently resting His hand on the back of my neck, Jesus softly whispered in my ear, "You are valiant, My darling, worth far more than rubies."

"I do not feel valiant, Lord. My weakness began to overtake my true desire," I confessed.

"Your adversary, the devil, will always be tempting you to worship his golden images, which take on many different forms, trying to lure you away from Me. But when your flesh and heart fail, My Strength prevails. I am forever your portion of Strength," said the Lord.

Pulling me away from our embrace to look into my eyes, Jesus continued, "Do not try to escape the troubles that come your way because I am using them to strengthen your foundation. You are being groomed to abide in Me and remain faithful to your calling. Avoiding the blazing furnace means you bypass the trying of your faith, which is more precious than gold. Each trial builds your spiritual muscle, and if you avoid what is in front of you, the next difficulty will be harder to endure. I am training your hands for war and your fingers for battle. The devil will flee when you resist him and surrender to Me."

"You are Good, Lord, and I will sing aloud of Your Mercy and Power. You have been my defense and refuge in the days of my troubles, and I delight in Your commandments. Give me the strength to endure the blazing furnace so those watching will see the Angel of the Lord standing in the midst of the flames, ensuring no harm is brought to me."

Comforted by 2 Corinthians 11:3; Matthew 4:3; Psalm 119:143; Psalm 37:39; Psalm 107:13,19; Daniel 3:13-30; Psalm 73:26; Proverbs 31:10; Psalm 144:1; 1 Corinthians 3:10-15; 1 Peter 1:6-7; Revelation 20:10; 1 Peter 5:8; John 16:33; James 4:7

17

longing to be seen

"It is rare to have one person in your life who will love you despite your shortcomings and fight to keep your heart from harm. My cup runs over because You blessed me with two people who filled me with such love and acceptance. But in their absence, I am left sitting in a void that leaves me longing for what was—a longing to belong; to be loved and accepted; to be seen and fully known. Who will see me now, Lord?"

"I understand the longing in your heart because I put it there," Jesus explained.

I turned toward the sound of my Savior's voice as He continued, "I created you with a deep longing in your soul, along with a need to be loved. Love is the most powerful element in the universe, so its perceived absence will seem immense. The combination of love and longing was designed to produce a strong desire within you to seek Me with all your heart because I am Love."

"I miss their human presence and their gentle strength in my life. Each day finds hidden sorrow within my heart," I replied.

"Will you let Me fill those voids for you?" asked the Lord. "I also am longing for love."

I was captivated by the vulnerability of the Son of God, and my heart clung to every Word as He continued, "My eyes constantly scan throughout all of My creation, looking for that one person whose heart is committed to Me. My eyes have landed on you, My beloved. Let me fill your heart with My Love and Goodness. Let Me show you My Strength."

He paused.

I held my breath. My eyes fixed upon Jesus, filled with tears as I heard His next words.

"I see you. Do you see Me?"

Comforted by 1 John 4:16,19; John 3:16, 15:5, 17:23; Psalm 107:9; Jeremiah 29:13; 2 Chronicles 16:9; Mark 1:1; Genesis 16:13; Matthew 5:8

18

clay in Your hands

"I always thought of myself as mentally and emotionally strong. But I now see a deep vein of fragility running through me, like a hairline crack waiting to burst open under applied pressure, Lord."

"You are My delicate porcelain treasure, fashioned by My fine workmanship, but you are not frail," said the Lord.

Pondering His Words, I felt something worrisome inside me. "I am concerned this weakness will cause me to fail and become ineffective in the purposes You have for me, Lord."

Moving toward me, the Lord placed His hands on my shoulders, continuing to comfort me. "I know you feel hard-pressed on every side, but you will not be crushed. I hold you strong by My Power, which far exceeds any other authority or force. With Me, all things are possible."

As I stared at the floor with my head lowered, the real fear rose in my heart as I asked, "Will I still be pleasing to You even with this flaw that hinders me?"

"Oh, My love," Jesus said softly as He lifted my chin, looking into my tear-filled eyes, "I sacrificed Myself so you can be whiter than snow, flawless, blemish-free in your spirit."

Taking both my hands, lightly kissing the back of my right hand, Jesus continued. "I am not finished with you. You are still clay in My hands, an unfinished piece of pottery. I use the fiery trials of this world to add layers of gorgeous detail to your original clay vessel. Each time you are re-fired in the world's kiln, irreversible changes take place within you, increasing your strength and endurance, softly blended with a meek and quiet spirit."

Jesus paused, tenderly caressing my palms. "My hands are mighty, but My touch is gentle as I transform you into a vessel of honor crafted for a specific purpose, both beautiful and functional. Do not lose heart, for I am renewing you inwardly day-by-day."

I was spellbound by the Lord's gentle but fiery eyes as He concluded with these words, "You are not a disappointment to Me. You are, in fact, My crowning glory."

Comforted by 1 Peter 3:4, 5:4; Luke 18:27; 2 Corinthians 4:7, 16-18; Isaiah 64:8; Song of Solomon 4:7; Ephesians 2:10, 5:27; Psalm 51:7; and 2 Samuel 22:33

19

giants at the door

Why am I troubled by the cares of this world, flinching at the "what ifs" and the unknowns? The enemies of my mind are emboldened by my weakened state. Giants whose names are Worry and Fear are crouching at the door.

"You have no need to fear those giants," said the Lord. "They may seem bigger than you, but I have given you authority to tread over all the power of the enemy; nothing will harm you."

Frustrated with my lack of bravery, I continued confessing my disappointments to the Lord. "Fear waves its fruit in front of my eyes, confusing my senses, seducing me to take the bait. The next thing I know, I am holding the apple and flooded with fear."

Turning to catch my eyes, the Lord said with a commanding voice, "Then drop the fruit and speak My name."

I stood there staring at the face of my Savior, His Words still ringing in my ears, piercing my heart. The room fell silent.

Jesus moved toward me, taking my hand. "At the sound of My name, your spiritual enemies will draw back and fall to the ground. They have no power over you, except what you allow."

The Lord's presence electrified the room, filling me with profound courage. "What must I do, Lord?"

"You are already saturated with My Spirit of Power, Love, and a sound mind. However, you must put on the full armor of God so you can stand your ground, which they will try to steal from you. They are waiting for the right moment when your guard is down."

Taking my other hand in His, Jesus continued, "In the spiritual realm, I have prepared a table before you, which contains everything you need to be victorious in battles. Your enemies were present at that ceremony, watching Me anoint your head with oil. They know who you are, to whom you belong, and the authority you carry in My name. Do not give the devil a foothold. They are counting on you being deceived and walking away from Me."

Grasping my head in both hands, mortified at the mere possibility, I proclaimed, "Oh no, Lord. I will drop the apple and call upon Your Holy Name."

As I looked up to gain reassurance from my Savior, the room was found empty, but my courage remained.

Comforted by Genesis 3:1-7; Deuteronomy 20:1-4; John 18:4-5; Psalm 23:5; Ephesians 6:10-18; Ephesians 4:27; 2 Timothy 1:7; Luke 10:17-20

20

loose gravel

"The ground below my feet feels unstable as I attempt to scale this mountain in my life. I am immobilized as I look out over the pinnacle with its avalanche of loose gravel, trying to negotiate my first step, Lord."

"You see unrestrained rocks, but those are chiseled pieces from the obstacle blocking your path," said the Lord. "I went before you, chipping a path across the ridge to prepare the way for your steps. I am your tether; give me your hand and keep your eyes on Me."

As I moved my foot side to side across the ground, pieces of rock fell from the cliff and out of sight. Looking up, I said to Jesus, "I am certain that my demise awaits my move."

His eyes fixed upon me, the Lord responded with a firm tone, "Things are not what they appear. You will either convince yourself of an insurmountable lie, or you will trust the Words I speak to you. You are safe in My hands, but it will be your decision whether or not to move forward."

Jesus stood there, never lowering His hand as I pondered His Words, hesitation gripping my heart.

"I am the Living Stone, building you into a spiritual house," Jesus continued, diverting my attention back to Him. "That obstacle in your path? It is you. You are the obstacle. Yield to the good work I am doing in your life, sculpting you into a perfect image of Me. You are My living stone, chosen by God and precious to Him."

Fear was fighting me on every side, but the Author of my faith was standing on the edge of the rockslide with His hand outstretched, waiting for me.

Inhaling deeply as if it was my last breath, I leaned forward, reaching for Jesus' hand. Courage flooded my soul when I felt His strong and steady grip as He pulled me toward Him. With the forward momentum, I took that crucial step of faith, my foot landing hard upon the loose gravel. To my delight, it was, instead, solid ground.

Comforted by Hebrews 12:2; Jeremiah 23:29; Philippians 1:6; Psalm 85:13; 1 Peter 2:4; Numbers 13:31; Psalm 37:23; Psalm 40:2; John 14:6

21

elusive hope

As I stare into the woods with a blank gaze, I feel hope drain from my heart. Elusive hope, appearing just out of reach, blocked by circumstances. My dreams are becoming faint images, no longer recognizable. "Are You schooling me in hope, Lord?"

"There is purpose in your suffering," the Lord said, sitting down next to me. "Be confident that your faith will produce a substance, proving your expectation of Me. Allow your suffering to fertilize the buried seeds of faith, putting your flesh to death and quickening your spirit."

My raw thoughts revealed themselves before I could stop my tongue. "I don't see any seeds. Just dust."

Jesus put his arm around me, pulling me close, fully understanding the tender state of my heart. "Patiently wait for what you cannot see—because no one hopes for what they can already see."

Pausing, giving me time to ponder His Words, Jesus continued. "Suffering confirms your spiritual knowledge and power and thoroughly completes the work I am doing in you. It will cause you to resolutely turn in My direction, producing a substructure that will support your foundation and join us perfectly together."

The thought of being perfectly joined to my Lord made my heart skip a beat. I felt a glimmer within my soul. Resting my head on His shoulder, I tried to soak up all His Love and

Compassion for what might lie ahead. Feeling a little anxious, I asked, "How long should I expect to be in this state, Lord?"

"You will suffer a little while," Jesus explained. "Hope in Me, for I am your portion. You will abound in Hope as I fill you with Joy and Peace. At the appointed time, I will lift you above the suffering and bring you restoration. Humble yourself and trust Me. I am your Messiah. I will deliver you from this trial and exalt you in due time."

Jesus turned to face me: I lost myself in His eyes.

"I am the Anchor of your soul. Wait patiently and bend to My redemptive time."

Comforted by Hebrews 6:19; 11:1; Lamentations 3:24; Romans 8:24-25; 15:13; 1 Peter 3:18; 5:6-10; Philippians 1:29

22

ashes for beauty

I began to realize that God was doing a work in my husband's spirit. An invisible, internal work with an eternal preparation.

Lamenting his ailing condition, I cried out to the Lord with a question but was immediately filled with fear about the answer.

"Are You preparing my husband for something?"

"I am preparing you both for My plans," said the Lord. "Your husband's earthly tent is wasting away. He is burdened on many levels."

Already laden with responsibility, my request seemed to come across with a tinge of pleading. "Give me the grace to be strong in the care and advocacy for my husband. Enable me to be a wise and noble woman as I conduct the affairs of our household."

Feeling Jesus' hands on my shoulders, I looked up into my Savior's eyes. His voice was soft like a whisper. "The time for care is drawing to a close. Your husband's spirit is groaning and desires to be clothed with his eternal house in Heaven, but his heart is still earth-bound with you, My dear. It is time to release him to Me."

I fell to the floor, weeping with the thought of losing my husband.

Jesus knelt down, meeting me in my pain. "Your sacrifice is sweet to Me, and your tears dampen My feet like ointment. I see your great love, but your work on earth is not yet finished."

The Lord continued as He slowly stood to His feet. "Be confident and do not lose heart. I have been preparing you inwardly, fashioned with intent for a future purpose at an appointed time."

My heart leaped as the Lord's voice rang over me. "You are an eternal crown of splendor in My hand, whose value is far greater than rubies. I will exchange these ashes for beauty. Rise up, My virtuous woman."

Comforted by Isaiah 61:3; 2 Corinthians 5:1-10; Proverbs 31:10, 27; Luke 7:36-50; Isaiah 62:3; Philippians 4:18; Ezra 6:10

23

what lies between us

The forest outside my window disappeared within a thick blanket of bluish-gray fog, revealing only the first row of trees. I know this landscape well, but it left me wondering what might be hiding behind the wall of haze.

"Have you placed a veil between us?" asked the Lord.

Surprised by the question, I turned to find Jesus walking along the back of the room, looking down as though He was searching for something.

"No, Lord," I quickly answered. "The veil that divided us was torn when You died on the cross and rose to Glory."

"Yes, I destroyed that veil," the Lord confirmed. "But you can fabricate another partition on your own."

As my Savior moved toward me, I realized He was waiting for me to search my heart. Hesitating, knowing full well what was clouding my view, I released a heavy sigh of defeat. Slowly shaking my head side-to-side, I inhaled deeply as if to invoke a thread of courage.

"It is fear, Lord." Drawing comfort from His loving eyes, I confessed, "I allowed fear to come between us."

Jesus swept the hair across my face, kissing my forehead like a mother who cherishes her newborn. "There will be many times when the uncertainties of life will be conducted from within a fog bank. Remember to use the Spiritual eyes I have given to you, keeping them focused on Me. Do not fear. Do not doubt, for I am only one breath away."

The Lord's Words sparked something inside me, causing my fear to fade. The fog outside was lifting, beams of light streaming through the mist with a rainbow of colors bouncing off the particles. Smiling at the beauty, I turned to share the moment with Jesus.

I was saddened to find the room empty, but it began to fill with Light as the Lord's voice rang out.

"Fear not, My child. For I know when you seek Me. I will always come to you in the storms of your life when you call upon My name."

Comforted by Psalm 44:21; John 8:12; Mark 15:28; Ephesians 2:13-14; Matthew 14:22-32, 15:16, 28:5; Deuteronomy 20:8

24

the Light Bearer's hiding place

The unpredictability of my life has planted me squarely in the center of uncertainty. This is not the first time I have been plagued with doubt, but I still found my heart being thrust into a place of secrecy.

"I did not create you to hide," said the Lord. "Quite the opposite."

Recognizing the Lord's voice, I quickly pulled the cloak away, exposing my concealed heart. "I am not hiding from you, Lord. I am hiding from this world that is too painful."

"I AM the Light of the world. No one can hide where I cannot see them, for My Light floods all of Heaven and earth. I know you feel battered by life, but its pounding force is shaping you into a golden candlestick, which will put Me on display. I created you to be My light-bearer, illuminating the dark skies of this painful world."

The smallness of my faith suddenly became a big reality, filling my soul with sadness and my eyes with tears.

Jesus gently caressed my face, His thumb brushing a tear from my cheek. Leaning forward as if to reveal a secret thing, I could feel Jesus' face scarcely resting on mine as He whispered, "I cherish the tears that flow from your tender heart. I keep them close to Me, contained in a bottle which bears your name."

Moving to the windows, looking out to the horizon, Jesus continued. "I know your pain and your wanderings, but a day is soon coming when your tears will be wiped away and everything will be made new. When the doubtful questions arise, run into the safety of My secret place where you can rest in the arms of the Almighty. My Light will remain bright from within My fortress, but any other hiding place will camouflage My True Light."

The Light was taken up, and the room became splintered with sunshine as I heard my Savior's voice saying, "Today you sow in tears, but one day soon you will reap in joy."

Comforted by Ecclesiastes 2:14; Jeremiah 23:24; Psalm 58:8, 91:1, 126:5-6; Matthew 5:14-15; John 8:12; Luke 8:16-18; Exodus 25:31; Revelation 21:4

25

the waiting room

Here I sit in the waiting room of life, stuck between what was and what is to come. Nothing seems to be happening in this place of suspension. The area is filled with people while I'm feeling strangely alone.

"It is more like a staging area than a waiting room," said the Lord.

"A staging area?" I asked, my question laced with dissatisfaction and fueled with restless aspiration.

"It feels lonely here," I continued with my complaint.

"You are not sitting alone," said the Lord. "I am always in the waiting room with you, and you must find Me here. Draw near to Me while in this place."

His warning rang in my ears as I looked around the room but did not see Jesus. I did, however, recognize His voice.

"A fearful heart will make it difficult to see Me, and it will cause a hindrance for the race I am placing before you."

As he addressed the anxious state of my heart, I began to see the Lord moving toward me from across the room. My entire being was seized by His presence, only to be released as I felt His touch upon my hand.

"Quietly wait on Me to renew your strength. I will do the renewing as you abide in My presence. Put your hope in My promises, which are waiting for you at their appointed time."

Jesus continued as He gently clutched my hands in His. "This location is where I assemble and ready my people for their next mission. It may appear suspended, but it is highly active. You cannot fathom what I have done from beginning to end, for I have set eternity in your heart. Wait for My instruction."

My heart now filled with anticipation, I replied, "I would faint in this place if I did not trust in Your Goodness, Lord. I will wait and hope in Your Word."

"Stand and do not faint," said the Lord. "Watch and see this great thing that I will do before your eyes. Wait for it because it will surely come. It will not tarry."

Comforted by Habakkuk 2:3; Hebrews 12:1-2; Acts 3:19; Isaiah 40:31; Luke 18:19; Matthew 14:24-27; Lamentations 3:26; James 4:8; 1 Samuel 12:16; Psalm 27:13; Deuteronomy 31:6-8

26

opposing forces

I woke up a prisoner inside my own mind, held captive by a vortex spinning up at the collision of two fronts advancing upon my soul.

"It takes two opposing forces for a storm to develop," said the Lord. "In My realm, Love is the greatest active Power, which never fails, unless you introduce another force into the mix."

Jesus' statement left me unsettled, already aware that I had interjected fear into my equation.

"You are asking me to move in a direction that feels risky, and it scares me, Lord," I responded, embarrassed at my weakness.

Drawn to that same weakness, Jesus moved close to me, taking my hand in His. "Fear is torment, and if you allow its strength to become the dominant force, it will fuel a disturbance in your heart."

Grasping my other hand, Jesus pulled me closer as He continued speaking. "You will either trust in My Perfect, Faithful Love for you or allow fear to be the object of your faith. I am always working toward your best interests, but you control which force will have the greater influence over you."

I stood silent before my Lord, keenly aware of my unworthiness, yet fully alive in my Savior's consuming Love.

"In the middle of the storm, I will approach with your solution. Watch with eyes of faith so you can recognize Me. Do not fear your next move. Whether you take the risk and step outside the boat or remain inside the boat, I will not leave you. I can work from either vantage point, but fear will sink you."

"You have always been faithful and gracious to me, even when my heart stumbles, Lord. I will trust you with my whole heart, for You are Love," I confessed.

Kissing my hands, Jesus started to move back from me. "What I am doing is obscure to you, but you will soon understand."

Our eyes were still locked upon each other, and the Lord's voice rang throughout the room as He disappeared out of sight. "No force is greater than I AM, for all Power in Heaven and earth has been given to Me. Nothing can separate you from My Love. Call upon My name to summon My Power, and I will show you My Strength."

Comforted by 1 Corinthians 13:1,8,13; 1 John 4:8,18; Romans 8:28,10:13; John 13:7; Luke 8:24; Matthew 14:26, 28:18; Exodus 3:14

27

abiding

A sweet smell is in the air as I stand, surrounded by creation. Clouds are rolling across the light blue sky, riding the Holy Spirit's gentle breeze. All creation is in flight, moving to the music of Your heart and swaying to the rhythm of Your Spirit as You sing over me. I am waiting for You, Lord: please meet with me to renew a Right Spirit within me.

As the rays broke the horizon, I could feel the warmth of the Son on my skin. The presence of My Savior was strong, consuming every part of me, leaving me breathless.

"Shhh," said the Lord. "I am right here."

I sensed the Lord's arms around me and His breath on the side of my face as He whispered.

"Release everything to Me. I heard you the moment your heart longed for Me, even before you called My name. I feel the desire in your heart."

"Will You stay here with me, Lord?" I asked, fully absorbed in Jesus' loving embrace.

Softly resting His cheek against mine, the Words of the Lord Jesus Christ settled deep in my heart.

"I will abide with you forever as you remain in My Love. After all, I am the One who chose you. I will respond to the posture of your heart, but always call upon My Name, which is far above any other name in Heaven and earth. Doing so is not for Me to hear you, for I am already aware. Call upon My Name so everything coming up against you will hear and bow their knee to Me. For I AM God, and there is no God besides Me."

Comforted by John 15; Zephaniah 3:17; Psalm 51:10, 91:15; Philippians 2:9-10; Ephesians 1:12; Romans 14:11; Isaiah 45:20-23, 54:17

28

depths of discontentment

The ground beneath my outstretched body was dry and strong with its earthy scent, my tears moistening the dirt as they fell from my cheeks. A steady wind caused the trees to sway in synchronism, echoing like rushing waters. Caught-up in my agony, I failed to notice the sounds of nature fall silent, succumbing to a shift in the atmosphere as the Lord appeared at my side.

My body tensed, and my breath became shallow as I felt Jesus touch the back of my neck.

"What troubles you, my dear?" the Lord asked, softly sweeping my hair to one side.

"My eyes fail as I look for your promises, Lord," I answered, face down and frustrated. "How long must I wait?"

A pause in the conversation caused me to lift my eyes toward the Lord for my answer. Standing there was Jesus, full of Compassion and Majesty radiating around Him.

"I see the depth of your discontentment," the Lord said, extending His hand. "Now rise to your feet."

Upon surrendering my will, Jesus touched my hand and set me upright, now face-to-face with my Savior.

"It is never wise to ask why the old days were superior to your current days, for it can quickly provoke your spirit to anger. Be patient while things unfold because the end of a matter is better than its beginning. I AM working in your good days and your bad days, training you to operate simultaneously within the two dimensions of abundance and suffering."

Humbled by His Grace and Kindness, I whispered softly with my eyes turned down, "Be gracious to me, as I am clay in Your hands, Lord."

As He communed with my heart and soothed every part of my wounded soul, I felt pride break within me and my spirit come alive as I heard these Words of my Lord ring in my ears.

"You are My witness. I have given to you this promised land on which you stand, but you must endure mountains and valleys to take possession. My eyes are continually on you, caring and providing for your needs. Is there any God besides Me? I will accomplish all that I please. For I am Alpha and Omega, the Beginning and the End, the First and the Last. Watch for Me, for I am coming soon and your reward is with Me."

Comforted by Revelation 22:13; Isaiah 44:8, 28; Deuteronomy 11:11-12; Philippians 4:11; Ecclesiastes 7:8-14; Psalm 119:58, 82-84; Daniel 8:18

29

manifested miracles

Sleep escapes my eyes as the clock mocks me, reading 3:00 a.m., my soul yearning for answers from The Living God. "Conflict is rising in my soul between my belief in Your faithful promises and the unfulfilled miracle that looms in my heart, Lord."

"I am Faithful and True," said the Lord. "My promises are not bound by your concept of time, and My miracles may manifest in front of you but remain unseen due to your distracted heart. The earthly realm runs parallel to the Heavenly realm, separated by one human heartbeat and a single breath. A person steps from this realm into the next, but My promises stretch across space and time. From My Sovereign position, I choose which domain My promises will be fulfilled, but be assured, they will be achieved."

I promptly felt exceedingly small within the expanse of the Lord's universe; my faith also reflected the same measurement as I replied with a meager voice, "I now realize the miracle may manifest differently than I originally envisioned. Give me strength to wait expectantly, never craving more while in the desert, nor testing You while in the wilderness."

Sensing my wounded spirit, the Lord moved in close to comfort me. I felt His hand gently caress the side of my face, resting under my chin, softly raising my head to meet His eyes.

"When you look with earthly eyes, you only see loss. Do not focus on the perceived absence of your desire, but, rather, focus on the inclusive miracle I am doing in your midst. Engage your spiritual eyes to see the multitudes around you waiting to be fed with only five loaves and two fish. Gather up the fragments you believe to be useless, for they are treasures of excess permeated with My Power, which you now hold in your hands."

I could not pull my eyes away from Jesus' strong gaze as I pleaded, "Give me eyes to see and ears to hear. Make my heart beat with Yours, Lord."

"I am the Faithful Witness, the Ruler of the kings of the earth, the God of abundance. I have chosen and called you to ignite and multiply those fragments, accomplishing more than you could ever imagine as I strengthen your inner being with Power. Be ready and surrendered to Me, for I will move swiftly at the appointed time. Be the miracle, My faithful follower. Future generations are depending on you for their miracle."

Comforted by Revelation 1:5, 17:14, 19:11; Psalm 106:13-14; Ephesians 3:20; John 6:5-13, 69; Hebrews 11; Ezekiel 12:1-2; Nehemiah 9:13-21

30

just out of reach

The sky was dark with the absence of the moon, a single star emerging on its vast canvas of space, twinkling to a tempo in silent rhythm. My existence felt tiny as more stars began to show their faces across the firmament. I shivered as the night chill settled upon my skin. The rawness cut through me, but my heart was numb to sensation.

The sounds of nature grew silent as my Savior appeared on the scene, His voice commanding yet soft toward me.

"What are you searching for among the stars?" asked the Lord.

Glancing over at Jesus, I trembled at His glory as He admired the stars as if for the first time. I was unable to form my words, and the Lord quietly took my hand and gently squeezed my fingers.

"Speak your heart to Me," Jesus said, softly kissing the back of my hand.

Put at ease by His Love, my confession poured out like water. "Everything seems just out of reach, Lord. I see potential shining in the distance, which lures me close, but my heart holds back, unable to trust the outcomes."

Placing His arm around my shoulders, Jesus directed my attention back to the Heavens.

"Those stars are the work of My fingers. I created the energy that fuels them and ordained their existence, each one named and numbered by Me. But My greatest work is being done in you."

Looking away, feeling a tinge of shame, I replied, "Life has wounded and splintered my heart. I fear that sliver has turned to dust, broken beyond repair."

Jesus pulled me close, whispering in my ear, "Is anything too hard for Me?"

I could feel the warmth of Jesus' breath on my neck as He spoke. My legs went weak, realizing that same breath spoke the world into existence. The God of the universe was concerned with a fragmented piece of my heart. Again, I felt tiny, but somehow highly valued.

"I am the Lord of Hosts who creates from nothing, to whom the whole host of Heavens and earth must obey. When I call unto them, they stand up together. Every cell, atom, and molecule will execute upon the sound of My voice and the Power of My Words. I will gather you into My arms as I command each particle of dust from your splintered heart to become whole. Keep your heart fixed on Me as you take hold of the Hope set before you. It may seem just out of reach, but I have prepared unimaginable things for you, which you will not understand. Abounding Hope is alive with Me because I am the Anchor of your soul and the Keeper of your heart."

Comforted by Hebrews 6:19, 12:2; Romans 15:13; 1 Peter 1:3; Luke 12:7; Proverbs 31:10; Psalm 8:3, 147:3-4; Isaiah 48:13; 1 Corinthians 2:9

31

undertow

The warning center sounded the alarm—a tsunami of grief was barreling toward the shoreline of my heart, generated by a disturbance and driven by a powerful force. Apprehended by the undertow, I was dragged into the open sea and pulled down into dark waters. My lifeless body hung in suspension while my mind bore witness to the silence within the aloneness.

My senses were disrupted as a shaft of light split the darkness and a sound penetrated the stillness, traveling upon the waters like a melodious lullaby.

The ballad attuned to my heart and called me by name, pulling my body to the surface, where I recognized my Savior's voice singing over me.

"Come back to Me," the Lord whispered in my ear as He cradled my limp body in his arms.

The spoken Words of Jesus awakened my spirit, my body aware of the betraying sand eroding from beneath me with every crashing wave on the shores of my heart.

"Peace. Be still," spoke Jesus, Son of the Most High God.

The wind immediately ceased, and there was a great calm across the earth's atmosphere and over the influences in my heart. My words escaped me, but the Lord answered my thoughts.

"I am here," Jesus said, rocking me back and forth in His arms. "I will hold you as long as it takes. I will not leave you."

Exhaling, I felt pain and grief leave my body as the Lord continued to speak Life over me.

"My delight in you is profound. You have set your love upon Me, acknowledging My Name and capturing My heart. I am your Mighty Warrior who will come to your rescue and protect you, remaining by your side throughout your troubles. All souls are mine—the soul of every living thing and the breath of all mankind lies in My hand. I will replenish and satisfy your longing soul with excessive goodness. Rest in My arms as I restore you."

Comforted by Job 12:10; Psalm 23:3, 91:14-15, 107:9; Jeremiah 31:25; Ezekiel 18:4; Mark 4:39, 10:13-16; Hebrews 4:12, 13:5; Psalm 18:16 & 19, 29:3; Zephaniah 3:17; John 6:63, 20:11-18; Matthew 18:12-13

32

the intersection

Here I sit at a crossroads in my life, idling in an intersection of decision, the signal before me glaring ruby red. Looking in my rearview mirror, I see my well-traveled, familiar path. It brings me a sense of comfort, but the streets are lined with grief.

Traffic moves around me as the light cycles in a methodical sequence while I remain stationary. The road directly ahead seems concealed, unsettling, and a little risky. I began to appreciate the beauty of an intersection, with its emergency escape routes to the left and to the right.

"What are you doing?" asked the Lord, interrupting my potential course of action. "You cannot flee from My presence, no matter which route you take."

Fully aware of Jesus' supreme power and authority, my flesh still rebelled, over-ruling any common sense and spurred on by fear.

"Turning left is very appealing at this moment," I responded with a small degree of sarcasm.

My attitude quickly halted as Lord Jehovah, the Spirit of Life, took my hand, interlocking our fingers, squeezing once— and then twice. I felt my fear dissolving in the presence of Jesus' perfect Love.

"You have an assigned purpose and plan, but it is down that road in front of you," said the Lord. "Turning left or right will only delay the inevitable and cause a skirmish between your will and Mine."

"I do not know how to do this, Lord," I said, with an honest and now humbled heart.

"How this will happen is of no concern to you," said the Lord. "I have already traveled down this path ahead of you. Everything is prepared and waiting for your feet to hit the ground running. I have you hemmed-in, ahead and behind, guiding and establishing your steps, working everything to its proper end. The only wrong step is no step at all."

My thoughts were racing as I stared at the narrow road ahead, the escape routes provoking me from both sides while flashes from my past streamed in the mirror.

"All paths eventually lead to Me, so the destination point is the same no matter your decision. But your choices will determine the length and enjoyment of your journey. Commit your decision to Me, for I am the Way that will lead to Life enriched with promise and blessing, no matter the hardships you encounter."

The Truth of His Words broke my fixation. Glancing over at Jesus, I found Him gazing at me with eyes of adoration. I felt the transfer of my Savior's courage as He squeezed my hand for the third time.

"The light is green. Which way will you go?"

Comforted by Daniel 2:47; Psalm 23:2-3, 95:3, 139:1-18; Matthew 7:13-14; John 1:1-18, 14:6; Romans 8:2; Isaiah 12:2; Jonah 1 & 2; Joshua 1:1-3; Proverbs 16:3-4, 9; Jeremiah 29:11; 1 John 4:18

33

stolen dreams

All feels lost as I stand before the Jordan River with my feet planted at its edge, the murky waters lapping at my toes. I watched my stolen dreams sink to the bottom, out of reach and irretrievable, a rippling ring moving out from the entry point. I felt hopelessness ascending to the surface of my soul, expanding like the rings of water.

"Were they your dreams?" inquired the Lord. "Or were they borrowed?"

The bewildering question shifted my attention to Jesus as he stood beside me, also surveying the waters.

"What do you mean?" I asked with a puzzled heart.

"Show me the exact place where your dream sank," said the Lord, pointing to the waters.

While surveying the location, I felt Jesus' hand interlock with mine, spinning me to face Him directly. Our eyes locked, Jesus reached for my other hand, softly brushing both against His lips before placing them over my heart and holding them firmly in place.

"The current of the Jordan runs fast and deep, but I control the living waters that flow from your heart. Make Me the object of your faith, casting My promises in the exact spot where you lost all hope. I will draw out your aspirations, for I satisfy the desires of every living thing."

"My hands of faith seem empty," I confessed, lowering my eyes in shame.

"On the contrary," said the Lord, "Your faith is very pleasing to Me. I see you keeping My Words and diligently seeking Me in all areas of your life."

As I cling to every affirming Word, tears began to flow down my cheeks as I was overtaken by the Lord's profound love, even in the midst of my faith crisis.

Jesus cradled my face in His hands, observing the state of my heart. I felt the center of my soul become still as His thumbs lightly brushed the surface of my skin, wiping away the teardrops.

"I sit enthroned above the circle of the earth. All things are held together by Me, the Creator of the universe. Surrender your dead dream to the One who swallows up death in victory. I will alter the components of that dream, making it rise anew, tailored to My purposes and doubling your portion. There is always a death before there can be a resurrection."

Comforted by Proverbs 20:5, 21:1; Colossians 1:16-17; Isaiah 25:8, 40:22; John 4:10; Genesis 1:1 & 27; Revelation 4:1; 1 John 3:22; Philippians 2:13; Job 42:10; 2 Kings 6:1-6

34

the embellishment

My footpath grew dark as the sun dropped below the tree line, long shadows extending across the forest floor. Darkness closed off all sides, and my feet were tangled among the dense underbrush as the path became concealed. No longer feeling secure, I froze along the trail, uncertain of my next step.

"What are you doing out here in the dark?" asked the Lord, grabbing my arm to reinforce my confidence.

"Trying to make my way in a dim and unfamiliar place," I replied, frustrated by the question—mostly because I did not have the answer I wanted, the answer my heart desired. After a long silence, I stated the real condition of my heart. "I am lost and cannot find my way."

"I know right where you are," said the Lord. "I always watch as you come and go. Do not be afraid of the unknown, for not even one of My children will be lost. You may devise your plans, but I direct your steps."

Listening to His voice brought peace over my heart and spirit. My body relaxing, I looked down as Jesus released my arm, noticing an object in His hand.

"I have something for you," Jesus said. I could not yet identify the contents, but I clearly noticed the piercing through His palm. The magnitude of my Savior's sacrifice on the cross elevated the beating of my heart.

Scanning my face as if to memorize its curves, Jesus glanced down as He opened His right hand, revealing a golden locket.

As He unlatched the lid, a brilliant light flooded the forest canopy.

"It is beautiful," I whispered, fully mesmerized by the embellishment.

"This is My gift to you," said the Lord, fastening the necklace around me. "An ornament of Grace to adorn your neck, filled with My Wisdom, Understanding, Judgment, and Discretion. A pendant to lie over your devoted heart. Wear it always because it will bring you safety. Follow Me, and you will never walk in darkness. For I AM the Light of the World, the Maker of Heaven and Earth."

Comforted by John 8:12; Jeremiah 10:23; Proverbs 3:21-26, 16:9; Psalm 37:23, 121:108; Luke 19:10; John 18:9; Genesis 3:9

35

broken pieces

Shards of glass lay scattered across the floor, creating a kaleidoscope of symmetrical patterns. Light danced across the walls as the morning sun struck the sharp edges—beauty in motion contrasting the stillness of my seemingly shattered life.

"Things are not always what they appear," said the Lord.

Picking up a jagged piece of glass, Jesus raised it toward the light, peering through it like a secret window into the Heavens.

"When your perception is splintered, reality becomes distorted. Things become twisted and deformed."

Watching my Savior sort through the fragments, I confessed, "I am having trouble finding you among all the broken pieces, Lord."

Jesus turned and caught my gaze, but I quickly lowered my eyes in shame.

"That is because your perspective has been skillfully diverted," the Lord said, moving toward me with compassion.

Touching the edge of my jaw, Jesus ran His fingers along the contours of my face, softly raising my chin to meet His eyes.

"You have been focused on the shifting patterns within your scope of vision and missed the enemy mirroring My movements. The Deceiver is highly skilled and knows human behavior well. Watch for him, for he is an illusionist."

"What must I do, Lord?" I asked with wide eyes and a concerned heart.

Knowing the fear rising within me, Jesus put his arm around my waist and pulled me close.

"Do not be afraid, for I am your Keeper. Your strength and confidence manifest when you sit quietly and abide in Me. Always call upon the Spirit of Truth and listen for My still, small voice. I will guide you into all Truth and show you things to come because nothing is hidden from Me."

Tossing down the piece of jagged glass, Jesus waved His hand over the scattered mess.

"Do not be worried about these broken pieces. The Heavenly Father has given all things into My hands. I will take all the shattered segments of your heart and make them whole again. My name is Wonderful. Touch the hem of My garment, and I will make all things whole. Watch as I unleash My wonders to your amazement. I am here, and it is well."

Comforted by Daniel 2:19-23; John 15, 3:35,16:13; Isaiah 9:6, 30:7 & 15; 1Kings 19:12; Luke 8:50; Matthew 14:36; Psalm 77:14, 121:5; Revelation 20:10

36

the tomb

For so long, my mind incessantly hoped for a particular miracle that now lies entombed deep in my heart. The stone has been rolled away from the entrance of the vault, but I fear looking inside because of what I might find. Will I only see an empty tomb, or will I pick up the linen fragments that lie upon the ground and trust the Risen One to make everything whole again? I have come to the burial place, looking for my Messiah. I desire to see the glory of God.

"I am here," Jesus answered, standing a short distance away.

Deafening silence filled the air as the Lord began approaching, eyes filled with Love and Mercy, focused only on me.

"I have been with you the entire time, conversing along the way. Was your heart not burning within you while we were talking?" He asked.

Jesus' intense presence awakened my spirit as He brushed my hair aside, whispering in my ear.

"I heard your breathing even before you cried out for your Redeemer. Tell Me what troubles your heart."

As the tears flowed and my body trembled, my answer came between sobs. "I was expecting You to bring the miracle to pass, Lord. I feel let down, even cheated, wondering where You were and what remains for me."

Jesus pulled me close as I wept and collapsed into His arms, the place where Love and Faithfulness meet together, and Righteousness kisses Peace.

"I am the Redeemer who stretched forth the Heavens and made all things. I redeemed your soul from the power of the grave, for My Love is the greatest force in the universe, mightier than death."

Reaching for my hand, Jesus interlocked our fingers. The God who satisfies the desires of every living thing was now strolling hand-in-hand with me. I was attuned to His every Word as He spoke.

"If you believe, you will see the glory of God. For there is no God besides Me and no greater Love than Mine. Remove the grave clothes that cloud your vision. Come with Me and watch what I will do."

Comforted by: Psalm 46:8, 49:15, 85:10-12, 145:16; John 11; Luke 24; Matthew 28:6; Lamentations 3:55-58; Isaiah 44:24

37

the healing

"**I see you in the distance running toward the sound** of My voice," the Lord whispered under His breath, hoping my frantic spirit would hear Him through the chaos of my heart.

"I feel the panic in your soul as you strive to bring the immobilized man before Me," Jesus continued. "I know your husband intimately and the state of his being, for he is one of Mine. I am familiar with your love for him but realize My Love is even greater. I have plans for both of you."

My breathing was labored as I reached the doorway, which was blocked with countless obstacles, keeping me from reaching my Savior. I started for the rooftop. Maybe I could get the Lord's attention from a higher elevation and lower my husband down right at Jesus' feet.

"There is no need to climb to the roof," said the Lord, continuing His attempts at breaking through to my deaf ears. "The task of lowering your husband is too heavy for you. Stop fretting; I see your faith."

My knees became weak, and my spirit quenched as I labored up the stairs, pulling my husband on his mat behind me. Reaching the top, I looked down through a hole in the floor to find Jesus looking up at me. His kind and gentle eyes locked with mine, but my body froze in the presence of His authority. The stillness of the moment allowed my ears to finally hear the Savior's voice.

"Come down to Me," said the Lord. "Leave your husband upstairs, for My angels have him in their care."

I hesitated to release my burden but chose instead to surrender to the Son of God. Making my way down the stairs, I felt a rush of extreme emotions and a strange release from within.

Waiting on the landing, Jesus took my hand in His. "Come with Me," He said, leading me away from the burdens that weighed me down.

"I heal in many different ways, unique to each individual and circumstance. Sometimes my healing is immediate, and other times it is not. Your husband's sickness is not unto death because he belongs to Me, the Resurrection and the Life. Do not be afraid; he will thrive on the other side, and you will once again live abundantly on this side."

Jesus gently brushed away each tear that began to flow as His Words settled in my heart.

"You will not understand My ways, so you must trust My Goodness. My earthly healing today is not for your husband. My healing today is for you, My daughter. Abide with me here and rest from all your good deeds. Touch the hem of My garment so you will be healed. Breathe in My Life so you can finish the purposes I appointed to you before time began. Is your faith in a healing miracle, or is your faith in Me?"

Comforted by Mark 2:1-12, 10:18; Luke 8:41-56, 22:29; John 11 & 15; Matthew 11:30; Romans 8:28; Proverbs 3:5-6; 1 Thessalonians 5:19; Psalm 100:5, 145:9; Acts 17:24-28; Job 33:4; Jeremiah 29:11

38

the prison

A secret place lies deep within my soul where fear lurks, waiting for its cue. Once sprung and no longer locked away, it quickly arrests my potential, locking me in a prison labeled inadequate and helpless.

"Who put you in there?" a man's voice asked from across the room.

Spinning in my virtual cage and peering between the bars, I could only see His feet, but I knew it was my Savior. I felt a mix of excitement and anxiety as the Lord circled, His presence vibrant and His steps intentional, coming to a stop at the entrance to my prison. I held my breath, watching the hem of His garment swaying in the doorway as I tried to collect my answer. The silence was deafening.

"My soul is disturbed. I am feeling ineffective and powerless," I confessed from within my prison, fortified with alternating bars of fear and shame.

"Where I AM, there is freedom," said the Lord.

I knew that was Truth, but my heart was struggling to believe. My thoughts were interrupted when Jesus' hand appeared in the doorway of my prison. The scars of His nail-pierced hands were exposed as He pulled me to my feet, our eyes making contact upon standing. His eyes were full of compassion, while mine were filled with shame.

"Do not allow your past failures, current experiences, or the enemy to confine you," Jesus warned. "For you are My light, and

I have placed you high on a pedestal to illuminate the room for those who enter."

As He gently caressed my hand, my heart found comfort as the Lord continued.

"You are My workmanship, clay in My hands. I authored your faith, but I am not yet finished. Do not fear who I created you to be, nor lower yourself to operate out of a mold not formed by My hands."

My body trembled as I pulled Jesus' hand to my face. I was overcome by His Mercy and Grace, and tears fell from my cheeks, pooling in His palm. Without a word from me, Jesus answered the concern in my heart.

"That shame is not yours to carry," said the Lord, kissing the back of my hand.

"I endured the cross to bear your shame. I AM the LORD who sits enthroned on high and possesses all Power and Authority. All principalities and powers tremble and bow before Me, and shame is held captive under the footstool of My Throne. You belong to Me and bear My Image. Be strong in the Power of My Might, for there is nothing powerless about you."

Comforted by Ephesians 2:10, 6:10; Romans 13:1; Luke 10:19, 11:33-36; James 2:19; Isaiah 45:18-19, 64:8; Psalm 23:5, 62:11-12; Hebrews 12:2; 2 Corinthians 3:17

39

no limits

Eleven floors up provided a prime view of the distant horizon, where my gaze was fixed on the unmistakable line between Heaven and earth—the marker between what is and what could be, what was and now is not.

"I stretched a measuring line across the earth and barricaded the sea behind doors," said the Lord, "but you have no limits."

I heard my Savior, but my circumstances caused my mind to flood with erroneous restrictions. My words followed the same vein as I retorted a little too quickly.

"Past aspirations seem lost but also mingled with the present: my soul is weary of this life. My spirit is tattered, grounded by…"

My statement was taken captive when large birds moved into my field of vision, hovering mid-air, appearing to tease gravity as they surfed the wind currents with little effort. I was mesmerized.

"You were saying?" the Lord asked, graciously pretending not to know the rest of my statement.

I glanced at Jesus, but my attention returned to the phenomenon unfolding outside the window. The visual had me spellbound, transfixing my spirit.

"Invisible forces, Lord," I replied, without breaking my hypnotic gaze. "My spirit is grounded by invisible forces."

The spell was broken, and my slumbering spirit awakened as the Powerful One drew closer.

"The Spirit opposes the things of the flesh. And all forces in Heaven and earth are under My Authority. Who has obstructed you from soaring to the highest heights?"

The rhetorical question crushed my already grounded spirit, for I knew the "who" was me.

Sensing my remorse, Jesus pulled my trembling body into His full embrace. I felt the wounds of my broken heart mend with just the touch of His garment.

"Do not presume to know the works of God or the way of the Spirit. It is My Grace that keeps you Heavenward. Persevere in the freedom I have provided as I renew a right spirit within you."

Releasing His hold, Jesus raised my head to meet His eyes, filled with Compassion and Grace, piercing to the depths of my soul.

"I am the Lord and Possessor of Heaven and earth. Watch as I show you wonders in the Heavens and signs on the earth. You will mount up with wings like eagles as I pour My Spirit upon you. I am not a God that stands far off. I AM here."

Comforted by Colossians 1:15-17; Isaiah 40:28-31; Acts 2:17; Mark 5:28; Proverbs 15:13; Psalm 34:18; Galatians 5:1-7&17; Ecclesiastes 11:4; Hebrews 4:12; Job 10:1, 38:4-11; Jeremiah 23:23-24; Genesis 14:22; Exodus 3:14

40

the silence

The treetop leaves were fluttering in the gentle breeze, clapping their hands in praise while the branches swayed to nature's celebratory voices—silent to human ears but glorious to the Creator. My spirit instinctively moved in unison, joyfully anticipating the crescendo.

A shift in the atmosphere caused the wind to cease, ushering in a different kind of presentation. The air hung heavy, laced with a sweet smell—all creation bowing in humble silence to their God. I knew my Savior was close at hand.

The warmth of Jesus' breath on my neck caused my skin to prickle as He whispered in my ear.

"The praise of your heart beckons me, My beloved," Jesus said, gently placing His hands upon my shoulders. "Your prayer rose before Me like incense, and your fragrance filled My throne room."

I rested my cheek upon His hand, and my breathing shallowed as I absorbed Jesus' Love and drew from His Strength.

"I long for the familiar tones of Your voice, Lord," I replied. "I sometimes fear You will be silent."

"You misunderstand the silence," the Lord explained, moving to face me. "I am not silent, but you are restless. You will hear me once you quiet your heart."

My heart bowed, and my eyes lowered as I stood before My Savior. There was a hush in the room as I seized His Words, planting them deep in my heart.

"I ride upon the highest Heavens, sending out My Mighty voice, the earth trembling when I look upon it. But with you, I dispatch My night song and draw you with My Lovingkindness. Awaken your spirit and listen for My voice singing over you. Move in unison with My song, for I draw near to collect you unto Myself. Arise and come away with Me."

Comforted by Song of Solomon 1:12&15, 2:10&13, 7:10; Psalm 19:1-4, 28:1, 29:4, 42:7-8, 68:33, 104:32, 141:2, 148:1-14; James 5:7-8; and Zephaniah 3:17

41

the Gardener

The transition between winter and spring is upon us when everything is withered and faded, while also hinting something new is at hand. I can smell the aromas unique to the season and feel electricity in the air.

"Like My seasons, you are also experiencing a shift," said the Lord. "Do you perceive the new thing I am doing?"

His comment stirred excitement for the potential contained within His words, but also slight anxiety for what it might mean. I replied with hesitation. "I sense you have planted seeds within the soil of my heart, Lord."

The pause in conversation caused me to turn toward the direction of my Savior's voice. Jesus was admiring the cut flowers I had proudly displayed in a clear vase, His hand gently touching the petals, like a gardener admiring the fruits of his labor.

I smiled as Jesus pulled a particular flower from the vase. His gaze still on the blossom, Jesus moved toward me. My breath was shallow as I waited for Him to speak.

"Your heart is My garden, filled with the seeds of My Words. Beware of the tares that have also been sown by the enemy. Let no one deceive you; starve those tares so they will wither and be swept away. My Words are alive, and My promises are set to germinate. Stay close to Me. Abide in Me. Remain in My Love."

I could not pull my gaze from the Lord's face as He continued speaking over me.

"I AM your Gardener. Your time of pruning is over. Forget all former things, and do not dwell on the past. I am declaring new things in your life, and they are springing up as we speak. I make everything beautiful in its time."

Softly smoothing my hair, Jesus placed the flower behind my ear.

"You are like a lily among thorns, My darling. Strong and captivating, you are the object of My Love. I have set My Spirit in your heart. Step out; it is now time for the harvest."

Comforted by John 15:1-9; Song of Solomon 2:2; Isaiah 40:8, 43:18-19, 61:11; Ecclesiastes 3:1, 11; Galatians 4:6; 2 Thessalonians 3:5; Luke 8:11; Matthew 13:25-38; Genesis 2:8, 3:1,8; Deuteronomy 22:9

42

living waters

Points of light glistened on the water as the sun's rays filtered through the forest. The rushing stream was music to my ears as I sat on the bank. The breeze—permeated with a warm, musty scent—tumbled the fallen leaves across the ground and into the waters. A sudden drop in the air temperature brought a chill to my body and an awareness to my spirit. I felt the presence of my Savior.

"I am mad at You," I said, unprovoked, my dream-filled hands clasped over the water.

"I know," Jesus said, crouching down next to me at the water's edge. His Splendor caused the beat of my heart to skip as His Compassion released my anger, opening my heart.

Studying the flow of the creek, tears streamed down my face as I cried out. "You are asking me to lay down all the desires You have placed in my heart. Your promises are all I have, Lord. My hands will be empty."

"Yes," Jesus replied, enfolding His nail-pierced hands around mine. "But then My hands will be full."

The truth of His Words caused me to look upon His face, His eyes filled with Mercy.

"I will help you. We will lay these down together."

I felt the Lord's strength pour into me as I opened my hands to cast everything upon the waters, but just as quickly, my hope began to diminish as the current flowed away from me, taking my dreams with it.

Jesus rose quickly, walking the creek's edge, His right hand outstretched over the water as fog began rolling up from downstream. I could not release my eyes from Jesus as I slowly stood, my voice silenced as I gasped for air, my hand stretched out to my Savior. As He looked back over His right shoulder, our eyes met for only a moment before my Lord disappeared into the fog. Holding my breath with anticipation, I heard my Savior's voice call out to me.

"I am The Fountain of Living Waters, and you have believed every Word that proceeded out of the mouth of God. You have not departed from Me, nor will I leave you. Watch the living waters, for I will return what I have promised to you, multiplied."

Comforted by Ecclesiastes 11:1 KJV; Hebrews 13:5; Matthew 4:4 KJV; Jeremiah 2:13; John 7:38

www.ingramcontent.com/pod-product-compliance
Lightning Source LLC
Chambersburg PA
CBHW050015090426
42734CB00021B/3284